That Further Hill

poems by

Macdonald Carey

Bombshelter Press
Los Angeles 1987

ISBN 0-941017-12-5

Some of these poems have previously been
published in *The New York Quarterly*.

BOMBSHELTER PRESS
6421½ Orange Street
Los Angeles, CA 90048

to Jack Grapes

CONTENTS

MY FIRST REVIEW

That summer I caught up with school
after spending a semester shipping out on a steel freighter.

We never made it around the world (just half way around the U.S.
From New York to San Francisco
Via Panama Canal).
I had a semester to make up.

I rented a room on the University of Iowa campus
from a Rhodes scholar and his wife.
The man was finishing up his doctorate.
They had a 4 year old boy who was brilliant
and precocious and obnoxious.
The boy was being brought up
by the gospel according to Spock and little else.
He was allowed to do anything he wanted
and was encouraged to speak his mind
even when not preoccupied with the Classics
(Like the learned Lipsius he knew Latin & Greek).

The locks were taken off all the doors in the house
and I couldn't take a bath in privacy.
The boy would wait all day and come in the bathroom
and sail his boats between my legs in the tub.
I finally blocked the door with a chair so he couldn't get in.

The next day he wouldn't leave his sandbox.
He spent all morning in the sand pile
chanting to himself under his breath.

He's declining verbs his mother says.
His father and I stake out
in the neighbor's yard
to overhear him.
He is saying the same thing over and over again.
"Mac Carey is a son of a bitch."
"Mac Carey is a son of a bitch."

HORACE

I'm coming home after an endless day at the studio.
I was in the beginning, middle and the end of the script.
I entered first and exited last. Six a.m. to seven p.m.
                    And I get up at four.
As usual it was the times between the beginning and the
                    middle and the end
that sucked my blood and sapped my juices.
I drive Sunset and go to Fountain to finesse the traffic,
cut back to Sunset on La Cienega and coast home to Benedict.
I compliment myself on my cunning and comfort myself
with the green shade of the trees on Lexington and the thought
there is no nagging wife or chattering children to grapple with
                    at home.
I am wrapped in total euphoria as I drive up to the house
                    and get out of my car.

A giant German Shepherd sits in front of my front door.
We stare at each other.
I walk past 40 doors and gates guarded by dogs snarling at me.
The Hound of the Baskervilles —
                    its jaws dripping saliva and blood
and Cerberus his fifty heads grinning at me.
But suddenly the German Shepherd gets to its feet, stretches
                    and wags its tail
Welcoming yet reproving me for being late.
I read the dog tag on his neck. His name is Horace and he lives
                    in Holmby Hills.

He has a phone number.
I call it and a machine answers. So I leave my
address and the message I have Horace in my charge.
Horace is hungry and I give him a can of Kal Kan,
provender left from my dead bloodhound's provisions.

Some of my bloodhound's (he's been gone five years),
some spoor must remain to have drawn this dog to my
doorstep, drawn him to this least safe house on a
traffic choked street where there's a car totaled
every year for twelve years. A bloodhound's spoor is only
matched by the lion's whose dung is so insufferable it
is purchased to frighten deer and coyotes and racoons away.
Mine is the only house in the neighborhood free from
intruding wildlife.

But something else is at work here. Horace and
I understand this and we understand each other.
He shuns the kitchen and walks into the library and
sits down in front of the poetry — the classical section.
He doesn't move till the front door bell rings.
It is the dog's owner.
Horace rises, walks out the door and into a vast
Cadillac in my driveway.
The owner thanks me and as he drives away I see
Horace sitting bolt upright on the back seat
every inch the major poet.

THE GOOD SAMARITAN

Father Lopez admits
he steals when necessary.
His homily Sunday was the story
of his Filipino father
who let a drunken marine
who'd been in a fight
sleep it off on his front parlor couch
and sent him off the next morning
with carfare to his base.
A homily on charity.

I told the good Father of my four days liberty
in Manila in World War II.
I am the youngest lieutenant in our group.
We have flown in from Mindoro.
Since I rank lowest I am sent off
to find a bottle of booze while the others
will wait for me at the apartment
Of a Miss Concepcion.

They are still fighting outside Manila
and there is a sudden blackout.
I head for the last light that went out
and knock on a door in the darkness.
I am admitted and asked my name and I say
I am from California, from Los Angeles,
from Hollywood I had worked at Paramount
and yes I know their son,
Charlie Gomorra who is a makeup man
for Wally Westmore and plays the ape
in all the Dorothy Lamour movies.

10

We spend the night talking.
The next day and the next night.
Then it is Easter morning and I go to mass
with the whole family and sit in the choir loft
looking down on a sea of mantillas.
It is the Filipino women. All their men
are off fighting the war and they
fill the church with black lace and faith and hope.

I tell this to Father Lopez and ask him
not to tell the story till I do.
He says he can't promise me anything
and reminds me that plagiarism is stealing
from one writer and research
is stealing from several.

CHRISTMAS SEASON

The Christmas season began early this year
with the theft of the traffic mirror,
the one I put up across the street to warn of southbound speeders.
It ends on Christmas day when the mirror reflecting northbound
speeders
is smashed by a brick.
The week before Christmas I work every day.
Monday I am rehearsing in my dressing room when I get a message
from the office.
It is urgent I call a Ralph Parker in Lawton, Oklahoma.
He says it is urgent. He has moved heaven and earth to reach me.
I call Him and Ralph Parker answers, "Your cousin Ed Clark just died.
Mrs. Parker and I been takin' care of Ed for years and he just
up and died. We want to get back our mobile home. But Doctor Pike,
Ed's foot doctor, has got himself appointed Executor and tied up the
Estate."
I don't know any Ed Clark I say, I don't remember any Ed Clark who's
a cousin.
"Well Ed used to talk about his cousin Macdonald Carey on
Days of our Lives and how old Mac's old enough to be dead but
there he is still playin' that doctor on television. You must
know Ed, he's worth 40 million and owns part of Wyoming, Mississippi
and Oklahoma.
His grandmother's name was Mahoney."
"Of course!" My memory suddenly comes alive. "I remember I had a
Grandmother named Mahoney."
Ralph says get a lawyer and hurry down here. Pike's got the
Estate and there's a million in cash in the checking account and
a million coming in every month from oil leases. I'm scared Pike'll
Get his hands on it — and he hangs up.
Well I call up my son Steve who's a lawyer in LA.
He gets a lawyer friend of his in Oklahoma City (a Spradling) to take
the case.
And that takes care of Monday.

Tuesday I have a message at the studio to call Spradling.
I do and Spradling says he has talked to Ralph that morning
and Ralph hung up on him after saying he had his 38 out and
was leaving

to blow Pike's brains out.
So we get to Mrs. Parker on a three way phone connection
and she says today's been a teary day. "I been here tryin'
to get to the beauty parlor — weepin' in my rollers.
I can't do nothin' with Ralph and Pike's made a pass at me.
We can't get a lawyer to get our trailer because all the lawyers in
town are busy with divorce cases."
Spradling says tell one of the lawyers it's Ed Clark and 40 million.
He'll put your case on the top of the stack.
Mrs. Parker says she will and to call Mr. Lamb
who's a friend of Ralph's. Now we call Lamb.
Lamb says he discovered the body three days ago with Ralph.
He was so excited he knocked over one of the piles of
crisp one thousand dollar bills stacked beside Ed's body which was
lying in the living room of his mansion which has crystal chandeliers
in every room — but no plumbing — because old Ed hated
water. Presumably because as an oil man he'd drilled
so many dry holes where he hit water not oil. Home is
where the heart is.

Anyway Wednesday comes around and we talk to Ralph again.
He has called to warn us Pike's lawyer is a man called "Cock."
Ralph's lawyer's name is Schwartzer.
Meanwhile we have discovered Ed Clark's mother and
my grandmother are sisters by the name of Mahoney and Grandfather
Carey who sold groceries to Ulysses S. Grant and Abraham Lincoln
married one Julia Anastasia Mahoney in 1873 in Galena, Illinois.
The other Mahoney girl married a Mr. Clark who moved south.

Thursday Ralph Parker calls again to say he went to Ed Clark's
funeral
"First time I ever let myself get near a Catholic church
I sat in the back row.
Still don't understand them rites."

Friday Spradling calls and says a second cousin showed
up in Dallas who's closer kin and rightfully claims the estate.

Christmas comes and New Years.

January 2nd Ralph Parker gets his mobile home.
I get peace
Though it is very dangerous getting in and out of my driveway
with both mirrors gone

IF IT AIN'T BROKE DON'T FIX IT

A guy I knows publicity agent
just gave a party
celebrating the dedication of his star
on Hollywood Boulevard.
The fact no one came to the party was headlined by the *Times*.
Publicity is a doubtful Aladdin's lamp to rely on.
I once did an awful movie with Shelly Winters called
"South Sea Sinner" where the *Times* reviewer
panned me. Wendell Corey was
awful he said. My publicity agent called the
Times and demanded a retraction. I got one —
the *Times* reviewer published a long piece apologizing
to Wendell Corey for having mistaken Macdonald Carey
for him.

OLD TOM

*"Depend on it sir,
when a man knows he's to be hung in a fortnight
it concentrates his mind wonderfully."*
                                        Samuel Johnson

It is Sunday and
I just saw Old Tom again.
He's 94 and he lies in his room
with the shades drawn waiting to die.
Sometimes he gets up when I come to see him,
but mostly he lies in bed and lets me draw the shade up
while I give him communion.

He keeps asking me to take more of his trees.
Most of his trees are gone now,
given away to friends and strangers.
But I say, "Not today Tom, I haven't the time today."

He has some kind of old world reverence for me
because I give him communion and he insists on kissing my hand.
I always protest but I let him.
Then I pull the shade down again and go.

Is it we're all partners now in waiting?
I no longer mind you kiss my hand at all.
But for that
the room is empty of us both.

I put off moving the trees
though now's the time for planting.
As if the putting off
could put off anything.
For that we hold
hands now.

VIGIL

The moment just before I go to bed gets shorter every year
The moment just before I turn out the light and record
The position of the bed from where I stand
My hand upon the switch

Started the habit of photographing the room in my mind
Just before I turn out the light
To make me feel at home in strange rooms
In strange or foreign places and to find my way
Or if there is a lamp beside the bed I make sure where
The door is before I switch the lamp off

But now I just turn out the light and don't check anything at all
As if I know the dream I'll have will bring me to
Other doors and other rooms
And other light.

SANTANA

The Santa Ana winds have come and
the world is clean again.
An old black and white movie changed to color
half way through and everything come alive.
Even the oleanders don't look dirty anymore.
The Standard station signs are bright blue and white and red
and billboards are slashes of color bordering the streets.
Yellow black and brown and green and purple.
Even the drab of the old Whiskey A-Go-Go
building has richness.

A redhead walks down the sidewalk taking
sips from a brown paper bag.
She keeps turning her head to the left
as if to brush something off her shoulder with her chin
or see something in the buildings she is passing.
Or is she trying to turn her face from the bright sun?
A man in a grey uniform is walking behind her
brushing things off the sidewalk into the gutter
which blow right back on it.
It is a windy day.
"A day to make you restless," I say to a girl in the elevator.
"A day to put you on your toes," she says.
I drive home after work and pine needles are in rows along the street
beneath their trees windswept clean.
Really not the day for birds to let their young
fly free from the nest.
But as a man said to me today
"If I didn't have horns I'd spread my wings."

The winds have been in my garden.
Umbrellas are inverted toadstools among the figs and roses
I swim a path through the cream of leaves that covers the pool
and dive for sunken furniture and children's toys.

HENRY BRACHMAN

Poor Henry Brachman died. I was on
my way to see him with some fresh fruit, the one
thing that seemed to spark his interest last week
when I saw him. Gave it to old Tom instead whom
I intercepted on his way to the Jordanian family
which lives nearby. 11 people in a
2 bedroom house in Northridge. The matriarch
of the family is threatened by death too — an aneurism
which will reach her brain any day. Tom is
giving them grape vines and a fig tree.
He is dying too and would have walked the two blocks
to their house if I hadn't shown up. The Jordanian
lady brings him food wrapped in grape leaves she
has been borrowing from him. Soon they will have
their own vines. It was hard to leave.
The Jordanian lady wanted to cook dinner for us
there on the spot. Tom tells me Lois admired a
dress she was wearing last week and she tried to
take it off then and there and give it to her. They
receive the death threats regularly — strangers in a
white white neighborhood. Not white as in
the milk of human kindness. They stand out
red and warm as blood on the cross.
The mass is not sacrificed on the altar alone
and Tom cantankerous as he is — how he shines
among his trees — his beauties as he calls them.
He's still giving them away to live as part of
him when he goes. I must get the quotation
I got from him — garbled as it was
something like "The followers of the dream will
be as worthy as the dream." That's not quite
right — but there's truth all around it.

But between yesterday and tomorrow
I think of the gift of fruit I was carrying
to a man already dead
when my car stalled at the mental sanitarium
where people are kept from the world.
Foothill Health and Rehabilitation Center it's called.

My car stalled and I phoned my service to get
the message Henry Brachman was dead and
as easily as shifting a shoulder bag
from one shoulder to another

I took that gift to Tom another dying man
who is giving his fig trees and grapevines.
His gift of fruit
to those who will live after him
so that he may live on.

This morning at mass
Msgr. Healy gave me Mrs. Sharpe to visit
at St. Vincent's Hospital.
Is she terminal too?
There is no end to this, I guess.

I'm turning on the computer.

GROWING

My boys are all 6'4"
And into their own lives now
We don't see each other much any more
I remember
We had a problem with one of them
He stammered
I kept trying to talk him out of it
(Speech is important to an actor)

The doctor said "Your voice is very
Threatening to an eight-year old. Tell him
You don't mean to sound that way."

I told him about my being an actor and all
And he never stammered again

One night after that
We were wrestling in the living room
After dinner
And I let him toss me over his shoulder

"There," he said
"I threw the whole father."

WE ARE EACH THE DOG

Inhabitants of the deserted town which surrounds us here
We are each the dog that will not die
But walks the streets past doors and rooms
We pant and tread a vectored path to a goal we never see
Our track the sidewalk curb from block to block
Through a town with no outskirts

If we'd look we'd see a cat run up a naked tree
And down again. There are no leaves to hide in
The leaves are in two piles and a child makes it one pile
And takes it away. The cat goes too

But we are the dog that cannot die and we walk on and do not stop
We are the dog that won't look around and walk with purpose
Straight ahead
We are each the dog that will not die and we walk on and on.

LIBERATION THEOLOGY

Someone brought his
stuffed dog
to church today

I asked the Monsignor what
church policy was in these matters

He said

As long as he doesn't
bark or bite

A NIGHT AT THE OPERA

When I asked the cab driver in
Mexico City why he speeded up when
he came to intersections, he said
"Senōr that's where the accidents are."

THE CHICKEN OR THE EGG?
THE EGG, OF COURSE

After many a summer
"He succumbed to the temptation to
Use his aesthetic judgment, he corrupted
The purity of commerical dealings
With artistic considerations."
He looked down from the height
Of his ambitions' ladder
And actually saw *the-fly-over-people*
Eye to eye.
He got dizzy in his inner ear
And it was then it was that it was
Hard to hear
Anything of meaning anymore
Just the sound of the gnawing of
The worm in the apple in the barrel floating
Over Niagara falls.
All a tumble intact into a safety net
Of taffeta and lace. The antimacassar on
The chair which is his coffin loaded with chotchkas
To the point there is no room for him
The ideas have gone out of these
Things he tried to take along.
The automobiles, the TV's, the Bomb,
The food stamps and the dildos
Possessed by his possessions he loses face
And headless, footloose and vacuum packed, winds up
Spaced out
Pure spirit sealed in a time capsule
Holding nothing but
The assimilated breath of every immigrant
To Los Angeles up to and including 1985
A man for every year is he

Who runs out of tracks in an old locomotive
Churning its wheels in desert sand
Burned out
A cinderfella
Eating up the time that's left
Chewing carp entrails
A simian facsimile
Spitting out the crumbs of hours
Crawling backwards on time's shore
Into the reptile's egg
To primeval ooze and
A Darwinian dawn
"Boulversé como las golondrinas
En la primavera"
Fowled up

THE GIRL

Suddenly
I meet her
we are both awkward strangers at the party
but
she makes it look easy
greets gargoyles, converses with druids
stoned to the gills in Milky Ways
oh the stars are out tonight stumbling over each other
while she dances as if she's skiing
bends in her dress to skirt the show
I can see it, hear its rustle as I look down at us
from above the air. No one knows we exist.

I knew a solemn girl who drove a Thunderbird painted tapioca and coated
in fur and feathers. A fuzzy car.
Not her she drives black
and red suppository up hills and down daily
gaily yet not smiling either.
She sleeps curled up in a coil of garden hose
on my back porch all sleek and curvy animal in a silver cacoon
or on a beach whose sand slops over the edge
into an hourglass double-timed by a digital clock
whose toes and fingers are being manicured — a thankless
job when no hands or feet are showing. Are they buried in the sand?

Black caviar, blini and butter are mixed up
in her yellow hair which catches in my throat and as
she dives off the gangplank I am treading water
holding out my arms to catch her
and she slips through my arms to the bottom of
the blue pool my home is surrounded by
and I never find her again
except in lenses of
telescopes and binoculars or
in frosted windows

I felt exactly like this once before.
I am in Spain doing a movie long after the Civil War
having a for me dazzling luncheon as an invited extra man
at the home of the banker who had staked Franco.
One of Franco's daughters is at the table.
After lunch we pile ourselves into Ferraris and Daimlers
and race up to El Valle de Los Caidos
that huge cathedral carved out of mountain limestone
both tomb and monument for the fallen
of both sides during the Civil War.
The place is closed to the public for us
and we enter the limestone cavern
and one of the luncheon party sits down
at the great organ and plays jazz

Tonight I am an extra man again in Los Angeles for a dinner party at
the Bistro
but first right now we are at the County Art Museum
the "A Day in the Country" exhibit
is being closed to the public for two hours for our group
the Heads of the Museum are giving a party a private showing
we park on the Museum grounds and are searching vainly
for the private entrance. A legless girl in a wheelchair
is in the parking lot. "Can I help you?" she says

HOW IT FEELS TO GROW OLD

How does it feel to grow old?
I don't know.
I guess it makes you
more aware of when you're wasting your time
or maybe just more aware
and just a little choosier about how you spend it
time that is
money and food and cars and clothes
and lots of other things
don't mean as much
but this moment
here
now
that's the ticket
that's it

But now I've said this
I realize I'm just as fond of
yesterday
and as for tomorrow—
I can't say a word against it
it's all of them that count
all of them that matter
yesterday, today and tomorrow
each and every one is important
Did I say all of them matter?

That's how it feels to grow old.

LIBRARY CARD

I just found a memo to myself here on my desk.
"Get me a new library card for Anna to use."
Anna is 90 and alone living in an apartment with my ex-wife
with no friends in this city.

My parents
every time I'd agree to take an enema would
reward me with an Oz book when I was a child.
And as I grew up I continued to reward myself in life with books
for every extra effort on my part.
It is surprising how worthy of reward you can find yourself.
My library now exceeds unreasonably my history
and the health of my mental state
and long ago outreached my pocket book.
Yet it is a crazy extension of me, not like the shell on
a turtle but a kind of tasty and edible roof and walls
that house me in a forest of doubt
where the children and characters that live in me
can sustain themselves forever

and

I'm going to the library tomorrow.

PACIFIC

I just found
This picture of
Me standing in the
Jungle in the Pacific
In 1943

Our squadron mostly
Sat out the war
Moving from island to island
The only
Thing I remember clearly
From three years
In the Marine Corps

Is the rat
That woke me
Every night
On Espiritu Santos

He wouldn't come
Out till I was
Asleep
And I'd hear him
In the dark

Waiting for me
To turn on the light
And see him
Sitting by the empty
Rat trap
Looking at me

The only bait
He ever took from
The trap I'd set
Every evening for him
Was a Lifesaver
He never touched
Cheese

I never caught him
And I never saw him die
He still
Comes out at night
And looks at me

LISTENING

I never sat down and wrote this before. I never
knew how to say it — ever. But I guess I never tried
before either.
But nothing — there is nothing to stop me now. No excuse,
nothing between us now but time not even regret. Time's
rubbed that out. Time's rubbed out shame.
I never told you I loved you Dad. And even if I'd said
the words, which I didn't, I wouldn't have convinced you.

The last look I saw on your face after you had opened
my door in a hotel at La Jolla to say goodnight.
I had broken my leg after too many breakfast martinis
and my squadron was leaving for overseas the next week.
You opened the door and almost hit the girl who was
hiding behind it.

I've forgotten many things about you but not that look.
That look on your face. That last look. It wasn't shock.
It wasn't disbelief. It was just a look of acceptance
of finality.

But there are other things I haven't forgotten too.
The careful way you carved roast beef during the only
moments of silence at the table that
held Mother, the Twins, Grandfather and always
a guest and me — when you'd ask me if I
wanted the fairy toast. I always got it because
I was the oldest boy.
Just another way you tried to make me feel
wanted since I felt the Twins, my younger brothers,
had taken my place in the nest.

After we'd eaten we'd all talk at once till
you'd quiet us somehow and say,
"Nobody ever listens to me."
But some part of us was always listening.
I kept listening even though I was way too
grown up for them by then — listening when you told

the same dumb fairy tales to the Twins.
They must have traveled deep into me
because the first night I was in Ireland staying in
the Yeats suite at the old Conna Inn
I took a walk in the evening mist and I swear
I saw the fairies.

And you fed me more than roast beef and fairy tales.
You fed me books. My reward after any sickness or spanking
was always a book. I read Mark Twain,
Stevenson, the Rover Boys, the Motion Picture Boys, Tom Swift,
the Oz books, the Horatio Alger books, detective stories,
Weird Tales, Dickens, Thackery, Edgar Allan Poe
and Captain Billy's Whiz Bang.

And you let me fill my room with all the smells
in the world. Before I collected stamps I collected
chipmunk and squirrel skins and rocks and marbles and
cigar bands. I remember Mother saying, "Charley, that's
too much. You are a banker, you know." That was
when you'd come home at night with a cigar band
for me you'd picked up in the gutter on 5th street
in front of the Pierce Building where you had your office.

You never came to Minnesota with us in the
summer though you'd sent us there. You stayed
home in Sioux City and worked through the summer
so we could go. Just as you'd stayed home from
college though you'd won a scholarship. You'd turned
the money over to your sisters so they could go.

You died that first year I was overseas
and I never told you I loved you
and that I listened to you

Loved you and listened to you.
Listened to you.

Listened to you.

THAT FURTHER HILL

Around the corner of my eye
I see
the space a door makes
before it shuts

at the bottom of my day
I live in that

narrow place
between my dream and waking

near you in the silence when the noise stops

as near you as horizon

and reach for a stone that
drops
in water

fish through my fingers

dust between my toes

there is so little time for waiting
even the flowers grow behind my back
I don't know when I stopped looking at myself
in the mirror

but I stopped long ago
and not from fear of what I'd see there
it's just I do not want to know
there is always time for that
and now

I know without looking

THE LATITUDE AND LONGITUDE OF HEAVEN

It only seems the wells run dry
No one yet's run short of tears
Inspiration's block no cause to cry
Don't blame your state on years

Youth is no longer wasted on the young
The young aren't older every day
Implant, transplant behaviour modify
Ripen, ageless with instant replay

The air forever holds the song
The image of the goal's the simple way
Faith eternally relative
But still to God we pray

How careful we must be to prime the pump
With water from the clearest spring
Though what comes out first is red from rust
The waiting's worth what faith will bring
It would be good to bring a cup
Your hands won't hold the stream
That gushes forth once it's begun
It overflows the dream.

BOOKS TO UCLA

I am donating my books to UCLA but they need indexing
Lois was doing the job but gave it up. She is taking
A course in thought transference and has ESP and a
Very psychic nature. As she went through the different authors she'd
Get these vibes just from handling the books. She got through
Beckett and Bellows and Burroughs with difficulty
Managed Durrell and Faulkner but when she hit
Gide she got ill. Graham Greene revived her but
Hemingway and Huxley did her in. She quit in the face of
Isherwood. Strange, there is a story if not a poem here
The aura of the printed word reaches through the cover of the book
So the books at Alexandria burned. Big deal. Who died?
Here in my own room in my own home on my own time
At 10 o'clock at night I am as free as any man can be
It is too late for most people to call and I have no lines
To learn for tomorrow
Every selfish bone in my body rejoices and loneliness is antichrist
Each aesthete, hermit, medieval monk and solitary had it all
When they had books and were alone with them
So the books at the Alexandria burned. Big deal. Who died?
I'll tell you who or who they tried to kill
The 10 million generations the first sovereign emperor of China dreamed
When he burned all books not dealing with
Agriculture, medicine or prognostication
The 6 million Jews almightly Hitler feared
When he first burned the books in Berlin
So the books at Alexandria burned. Big deal. Who died?
Not them they are around me now
The Phoenix is alive and well. And so am I.